YOUR KNOWLEDGE HAS VALUE

Timo Höllein

Women in Modern Times

GRIN Verlag

Bibliografische Information der Deutschen Nationalbibliothek:

Die Deutsche Bibliothek verzeichnet diese Publikation in der Deutschen National-
bibliografie; detaillierte bibliografische Daten sind im Internet über http://dnb.d-
nb.de/ abrufbar.

Imprint:

Copyright © 2010 GRIN Verlag GmbH
Druck und Bindung: Books on Demand GmbH, Norderstedt Germany
ISBN: 978-3-656-54276-6

This book at GRIN:

http://www.grin.com/en/e-book/264733/women-in-modern-times

GRIN - Your knowledge has value

Der GRIN Verlag publiziert seit 1998 wissenschaftliche Arbeiten von Studenten, Hochschullehrern und anderen Akademikern als eBook und gedrucktes Buch. Die Verlagswebsite www.grin.com ist die ideale Plattform zur Veröffentlichung von Hausarbeiten, Abschlussarbeiten, wissenschaftlichen Aufsätzen, Dissertationen und Fachbüchern.

Visit us on the internet:

http://www.grin.com/

http://www.facebook.com/grincom

http://www.twitter.com/grin_com

Women in Modern Times

An article about the progress that has been made in the emancipation of women from the 16th to the 21st century, remains of "gender roles" nowadays and the differences in the idea of women in western and eastern civilisations.

Throughout history, women have traditionally been regarded as inferior to man in both power and status. As in Elizabethan times, in all societies the obvious biological difference between women and men is used as justification for forcing them into different social roles which limit and shape their attitudes and behaviour.

A common view was that wives should obey their husbands and daughters should be ordered about by their fathers. The Elizabethan idea of a woman was clearly defined as a faithful housewife and mother, blessed by God with many children.

A daughter was dependent on her father until the age of marriage and thenceforth bound to her husband for the rest of her life. Marriages could neither be lawfully divorced nor could legal annulments be considered, due to the high value of a woman's purity. If a woman separated from her husband, she was literally blemished, despised by society and forced to live a life as a single until she died.

Furthermore women were not allowed to go to school or university, perform work or earn money and since they officially were not just an emotional belonging, but physical property of a man, a father or husband was allowed to chastise them if necessary. Nonetheless, during the Elizabethan era women (in England) enjoyed more privileges than at any other time of the following centuries (except the 21st).

Even though men seemed to have more preferences, women were not obliged to give birth to a boy rather than a girl: any child was appreciated and seen as a blessing of God regardless of the gender.

Despite the prohibition to go to school or university, many (noble) women were tutored privately and therefore very educated, sophisticated and skilled in many occupations. Besides, while men were allowed to chastise women, they were in fact not allowed to harm or humble women in any way.

In the following centuries the idea of women changed, at first it worsened, later it improved, but generally the circumstances were stacked against women.

Since the early days of the Industrial Revolution women in western civilisations were exploited, denounced and generally disadvantaged – especially in the field of work.

The newly introduced factory system swapped the prohibition to work with the necessity to drudge for a minimum wage, much lower than a man's pay for the same occupation.

A woman's "low" economic value forced her to work several additional hours a day to contribute her substantial share to the family. In addition to an exhausting occupation in a factory, a woman also had to give birth to, raise and take care of several children.

But still, the emancipation of women continued even during the darkest age of mankind. While women of the lower class barely had enough time to be a mother and earn enough money to pay the actual living expenses , women of the middle and upper classes were increasingly confined to the home with little to do except to take care of their children. Many of these idle women became critical of their position in society and actually found time to devote themselves to various religious and moral causes and even to become interested in substantial changes like the women's rights movement.

Eventually, both working-class and bourgeois women insisted on change and contributed to the advancement of feminism.

In the late 20th and early 21st century, the emancipation of women reached its peak for now (in western civilisations).

The idea of a woman in Modern times is a lot different of what it was back in the 16th century.

Nowadays, women can decide themselves whether and whom they want to marry, how many children they want to have and when they want to become a mother.

Women are no longer bound to a man since their first day of life and can express their individuality, thus make their on decisions and live their lives without the constant approval of men.

In general women have the same chances of education as men and are also allowed to perform any profession they want to (and can qualify for).

Unlike in former times, women are allowed to vote and have the same rights to participate in political, social and economic matters just as men.

The "gender roles" of ancient generations aren't clearly defined anymore and women are no longer (obviously) inferior to men or disadvantaged just because of the difference in gender.

Yet our society has to face remains of former ideologies that influence our daily life on an unequal basis. Even though a woman is allowed to choose her life partner freely, she still carries (and always will carry) the burden of giving birth to a child, which is unfairly at her disadvantage and ultimately results in job-related inequalities.

A woman may be free to choose any profession she wants to, but due to the fact of possible pregnancy, maternity leave and other child-related unavailability time, a woman generally earns less money compared to a man of the same profession.

Although a woman is not bound to a man anymore as she used to be and even though she won't be despised by society anymore for leaving her partner (or her partner leaving her), as an expectant mother and the first 2 to 6 years of maternity, a woman is heavily limited in her means to earn money and sustain her standard of living.

In most of the cases (of separated couples) the father abdicates from his responsibility for his children and leaves the mother with the task to live a life as a mother, a housewife and an employee.

This often places a woman in a position of having to make a difficult decision: either they choose to stay in an uneasy relationship to avoid financial insecurities (mostly for the well-being of their children) or they decide to be a single mother with all of its burdens and still try to make the best of it.

However, both of the decisions place a woman in a disadvantaged position, which in any way deters her from a professional career and ultimately is responsible for worse job perspectives and lower wages.

Today's idea of women in western civilisations is a mixture of the Elizabethan idea of a woman and women during the Industrial Revolution, slightly adjusted to attributes of the present time:

Women still do most of the housework, are still primarily responsible for their children and still carry more burdens of the everyday life than man do, while they still work for less payment and have less career perspectives. Nevertheless the situation greatly improved compared to past centuries and remaining inequalities will soon to be no more due to steadily advancing feminist movements – at least in western civilisations.

After all we must not forget that the relatively liberated and affluent women of industrialised countries are only a small minority of women in the world today. Women in many non-western countries, and especially in the so-called Third World generally live in a state of subjection and misery. Most of their vitality is consumed by a hard and grim struggle for mere survival. Discussions about "sexual liberation" shaped by western impressions sound, at best, irrelevant, and at worst, unreliable to them. In nearly all "underdeveloped" countries women suffer from circumstances that are very similar to those during the Industrial Revolution: they live in poor, rural areas, are illiterate, malnourished, exhausted and forced to work long hours for little reward.

Furthermore influences from other centuries shape the idea of women in these countries as well: boys are favoured over girls from the moment of birth, they get better education, clothes and food. Woman have generally less rights and are early given away in marriage without being able to do anything about it. Gruelling work and constant pregnancies keep them weak and dependent, while any attempt to improve their situation bears consequences that makes it even worse.

In a nutshell, today's women living in the Third World live a life that seems to be worse than the life of women in western civilisations in any of the past centuries.

The emancipation of women hasn't been completed yet and as long as the equality of men and women isn't secured all over the planet, injustice will dominate people's lives and probably their minds as well.